CONFESSIONS OF A SOUTHERN BABY-BOOMER

*How I Survived Crack Cocaine Addiction,
the Mafia & Other Totally True Tales*

Meg Henderson Wade

Cover illustration by Lowell Hildebrandt

authorHOUSE®

AuthorHouse™
1663 Liberty Drive
Bloomington, IN 47403
www.authorhouse.com
Phone: 1-800-839-8640

First published by AuthorHouse   5/19/2010

ISBN: 978-1-4520-2652-7 (e)
ISBN: 978-1-4520-2651-0 (sc)

Printed in the United States of America
Bloomington, Indiana

This book is printed on acid-free paper.

IT WAS A DARK AND STORMY NIGHT AND I WAS BORN ON A FULL MOON...

I WAS BORN IN ATLANTA AND MY MOTHER'S NAME IS DIXIE.

HOW NAÏVE CANS A SMALL TOWN GIRL WHOSE MOTHER'S NAME IS DIXIE BE?

WELL, READ ON, AND, TO QUOTE BETTE DAVIS, " FASTEN YOUR SEATBELTS—IT'S GOING TO BE A BUMPY RIDE"!! AS THEY SAY "TRUTH IS STRANGER THAN FICTION."

My friends have told me since I was in my twenties that I need my own mini-series. Well, truth is stranger than fiction, especially in my case. Of course, I'm somewhat of a Drama Queen. I mean I hadn't decided to be a Drama Major in college for nothing!! I used to be so bummed that I hadn't suffered enough in life to be a great actress—well, Gosh Darn it, I have suffered some of life's realities. I now feel the need to tell my story to hopefully help someone else navigate the trials and tribulations of
DRUG ADDICTION.

I used to be embarrassed about being from a small hick town known for NASCAR racing. Then it grew to be one of the biggest sports around. So, twice a year, thousands of fans invade the small town of Martinsville, Virginia and there isn't a motel to be found vacant. I mean even The Fairstone Motel and The Dutch Inn are booked solid!

Do you know why bootleggers first jacked-up their cars' rear ends? Junior Johnson who was immortalized by Jeff Bridges in the movie "The Last American Hero", used to jack up the back end of his car so that when he drove around rural roads with jars of moonshine in the trunk, the car would look normal.

My mother, Dixie, and my future mother-in-law were extras in this movie that was filmed partially at the Martinsville Speedway. Jeff Bridges, Gary Busey and Valerie Perrine starred and a 12 year old yours truly appeared in this flick that is still played on late night cable channels.

Like we always said, "Liquor by the Drink will never come to Martinsville—Hell, The Baptists and the Bootleggers won't allow it". Hey, I was raised southern Baptist, so I can say H-e-double toothpicks if I really, really mean it.

Well, bless your heart, for thinking that I just throw curse words around at the drop of a hat. We Southerners hate to be though of as rude. I just adore that ole Southern saying, "Bless your Heart". You can get away with almost anything if you say, "Bless your Heart" before or after it.

And to paraphrase another famous Southern Belle, Blanche DuBois, "I have always depended on the kindness of strangers", Bless Your Heart.

WELL, PUT ON YOUR SEATBELTS

AND LISTEN TO HOW

A SOUTHERN BELLE
SURVIVED
COCAINE ADDICTION,
THE MAFIA,
&
OTHER TOTALLY TRUE TALES

"You know I think her hairdresser was on drugs when he fixed her hair, bless her heart. Why, Myrtle, I've always liked your Major Bouffant Do!!"

It kind of takes the sting out of an insult and you can get away with all sorts of stuff you shouldn't.

Southern Shtick!!

CHAPTER TWO

I was born in Atlanta and my mother's name is Dixie.

Dixie's parents ran the local BBQ restaurant named "The Dixie Pig".

Now, Grandma Margaret swore that my Mom was named after Dixie Crosby, Bing Crosby's first wife. And that's another charming Southern habit—naming your child after a celebrity!! I mean how many Shirley's, Joan's and Britney's do we have running around now?

Hmm, I rest my case.

I was named Margaret and have always gone by <u>Meg</u>. Of course, I was named after my Grandmother Margaret. She was one of the few people who was named Margaret and went by Margaret. Did you know that Margaret Mitchell's nickname was Peggy?

Grandma Margaret always adored being called Margaret.

Being a Baby-Boomer, all I could think of was the Dennis the Menace TV show and that smarty-pants girl named Margaret that everyone loved to hate.

No thanks I will stick with **MEG**. It suits me—cute, perky, and not too serious and hey, its only 3 letters, so when I have something monogrammed, it spells out my entire name—love it!!

I wasn't always proud of my Southern, Dixie-born (pun intended) heritage. When I was about 8 years old I used to feel bad that I wasn't "ethnic". Hey I wasn't Italian, Jewish or black. I was a boring WASP (White Anglo Saxon Protestant) with a southern accent.

Boy, was I glad when the movie, "Steel Magnolias" came out!! Finally, I had vindication that yes we quirky, unique Southerners did have our own ethnic thing going on!

Hey Dolly Parton, "Laughter through tears is my favorite emotion", too!! And following in Dolly's footsteps, no self-respecting Southern lady would even think of leaving the house without her hair and make-up done.

Because, as my hairdresser used to say,
"You may just meet your future"
on the way to the Piggly Wiggly.

And hey, here's a big southern shout out to Larry, the Cable Guy and his famous "git r done" phrase! My New York friends just think he is such a hoot. I personally don't "git" it. I mean all the guys from Martinsville dressed in plaid shirts and shouted "git r done". That was my norm!! So, I guess we Southerners have truly arrived now—we have our own ethnic stereotypes—Grandma Margaret would be so proud!

BLESS YOUR HEART

CHAPTER THREE

Now, Grandma Margaret—there's a real Steel Magnolia. She was divorced in the sixties and opened a new restaurant after she turned over The Dixie Pig to her curb boy, Gary, who still runs it today. The new diner was named The Dinner Bell. She ran that diner like Scarlett ran the lumber mill.

Nothing escaped her watchful eye. She would charm all the customers and vendors with her sweet smile and knowing laugh!!

Grandma Margaret had a gumball machine in the diner that held only one, speckled gumball. And if you were lucky enough to get that very, special speckled gumball---

You Won A PONY!!!

Oh, the dreams I had of winning a Pony. Just like Ralphie in the movie, "A Christmas Story", wanted to get an official Red Ryder hundred-shot model air rifle---I Wanted A PONY!!!

Alas, my PONY dreams went the way of Ralphie's Red Ryder Rifle— Gone With The Wind. And for a girl who was born in Atlanta whose Mother's given name was Dixie, well the irony was indeed clear.

In her heyday, Grandma Margaret was known as a fine, southern woman. Then the fickle finger of fate (for you non baby-boomers, that's from Laugh-In in the 1960's) swooped in and Grandma Margaret began to change. It was Alzheimer's. The funny, okay ironic, thing about Alzheimer's disease is that a person doesn't just suddenly start to forget everything overnight. It's about a twenty year- long progression of one depressing change after another. My family and I used to joke, "Hell, I wish she'd forget something and stop being so hateful, bless her heart."

She started to get very paranoid like everyone was out to cheat her. I can assure you, the handyman who did odd jobs for Grandma Margaret really was not stealing the prisms from her Chandelier!! It reminded me of Scarlett O'Hara once again hanging onto her beloved Tara and her Southern history. Save my Chandelier from the Yankees!!

When Grandma Margaret died,
My own Mom, Dixie gave me
Some of her chandelier prisms
So I can continue to hang onto
My own piece of Tara
And Grandma Margaret.

CHAPTER FOUR

CONFESSIONS OF AN ALMOST SOUTHERN MAFIA PRINCESS

Just to give you another example of how naïve a small town Southern girl whose mother's name is Dixie can be. I was about twenty-three years old and met a man in Atlanta, Georgia whose name was Alberto Romano (The name has been changed to protect moi!). Alberto and I met in a theatre where we were both apprentices at the Academy Theatre's Apprenticeship Program in Atlanta.

*He told me his grandfather was the **"Don of Buffalo"** and I asked, "Oh, you mean his first name is **Donald?"***

I was serious as a heart attack. This was 1983 and I had no idea about the movie, "The Godfather" or "Goodfellas" nor any other Mafia movies.

Okay, another interesting Confession from a Southern Baby-Boomer. Unbeknownst to little ole' naïve me, his grandfather, Alberto Romano was known as "The Grandfather of the Cosa Nostra" and he ruled Niagara Falls, New York and was in power for over fifty two years in upstate New York and Canada....

THE CONFESSIONS CONTINUE...

Little was known about Don Alberto until recently a book was written by Mike Rizzo. There are even tours coordinated by The Mob Tours in Niagara Falls today where he gives a 90 minute tour of the life and escapades of Alberto Romano and how the FBI tried for decades to take him out.

One place of special interest to me and obviously many others on the tour, would be the "Romano Memorial Chapel". This is where Don (Hey, it doesn't mean Donald!!) Alberto worked for many, many years and his nickname was "The Undertaker."

In fact, when my mother, Dixie, heard about my boyfriend and that he was originally from Niagara Falls, New York, she naively told a friend of hers who was also from Buffalo, New York.

Her friend replied, "Dixie, don't you know what the Romano Memorial Chapel does? They double bury the bodies in the casket. You may think your Aunt Helen is going to her final resting place alone; however, Good Fella Vito may be buried underneath her because he lost a bet with the Romano bookie."

Needless to say, this story was repeated to me very dramatically by my mother. And, of course she was worried for me. I guess she just didn't want to think of me as being "Married to the Mob".

Meanwhile back at the Academy Theatre in Atlanta, Alberto and I were in rehearsals for a play, "Playground" written and directed by Kenny Leon.

Kenny Leon is known for the Tony-award winning revival of "A Raisin in the Sun" which starred Phylicia Rashad and Sean 'P. Diddy' Combs. In fact some very impressive people attended our production of "Playground"— Yolanda King, Martin Luther King's daughter, and Freddy 'Boom Boom' Washington from Television's "Welcome Back Kotter."

The play was performed at the Martin Luther King Center for Non-Violent Social Change. Of course, it's a lot easier to answer the phone with just "The King Center" even though all of the history of The King Center is definitely a big deal in American history.

Barbara Lebow of The Academy Theatre also produced another award-winning, Broadway bound show, "A Shayna Maidel". The play tells the story of a Jewish girl in New York during the holocaust. I was blessed to be able to be at the world premiere of "A Shayna Maidel" which was produced by The Academy Theatre in 1985.

I am thrilled to be a part of this rich theatre history and Alberto and I played opposite each other in Kenny Leon's play, "Playground".

I fell head over heels in love and the feeling was evidently mutual. I was twenty three and Alberto was thirty seven. One day Alberto told me he had separated from his wife. I was surprised and pleased because we had been flirting.

What I didn't know was that if someone was married and Mafia, they don't usually leave their wives! And I also didn't realize that Alberto's wife's background was also "La Familia".

Alberto used to drive a beautiful turquoise Porsche 911 that he would park outside of my apartment building when he would visit me. Sometimes his car would be broken into and the love notes I had written him would have been stolen.

He took me to the movie, "Prizzi's Honor" and I was very aware of the irony of the plot—a WASP falls for a Mafia man. It was really strange, yet we didn't acknowledge the fact very often that his family was infamous.

Throughout the years, Alberto and I would see each other every couple of years just like the movie with Alan Alda and Ellen Burstyn, "Same Time, Next Year". One time we both drove six hours and we met in Gaffney, South Carolina—home of the Giant Peach just off interstate 85.

As I grew older and I thought back on these episodes, I realized that someone was keeping tabs on Alberto while he was at my apartment. This was actually very scary when I realized this. At the time, my ignorance was bliss! Way back in the 1980's, we didn't have the internet to do research like we do now, so I didn't know that my friendship with Alberto Romano was as dangerous as it was.

Alberto finally got divorced to be with me and I ran away back to Martinsville to my roots and to help look after my Mom, Dixie, who had just been diagnosed with breast cancer. I decided that I really didn't want to live life as a Southern Mafia Princess so I tested Thomas Wolfe's advice of "You Can't go Home Again."

CHAPTER FIVE

I LEFT MY HEART IN SAN FRANCISCO

I grew up in the 1960's and 1970's. Of course, like most of us baby-boomers, I had done Marijuana or "Mary Jane" as I liked to call it, drank some, tried a little cocaine in the 1980's but hey, I'd never had an addiction problem with any of it. Mary Jane made me paranoid and shy—and with my out-going personality that was definitely no fun for me. I had it all figured out. The way I felt when I smoked marijuana was the way most people felt in normal social situations—shy and paranoid.

I was "High on Life" and didn't need artificial stimulants –other than my favorite Diet Dr Pepper! As one of my favorite college drama professors, Uncle Vernon, used to say, "Dr. Pepper is one molecule away from plastic." Well, all I can say is I like to drink Dr Pepper at 10, 2, and 4 and didn't Dustin Hoffman say in "The Graduate" that plastics are the future?

I was a girl from a small southern town—Martinsville, Virginia and then I went to college at Appalachian State University in Boone, North Carolina. I couldn't afford to go to college anymore so I did what any girl who has every lived in a small southern towns does, I dropped out of college and moved to the Haight Asbury section of San Francisco. I was either nuts or ballsy or a little of both. And thus another mini-series episode begins....

SAN FRANCISCO

Straight from LA—Lower Axton, Virginia to the Castro District in San Francisco. I had been a drama major at Appalachian State University and a friend of mine from High School was gay and the Castro District was his Mecca and seemed like the perfect destination for two artsy, adventurous small towners. We moved there right after Harvey Milk and Mayor Moscone had been assassinated and Diane Feinstein was just named Mayor. Wow, history in the making and I was right in the middle of it— wow, sure beats cow-tipping in LA- Lower Axton.

You would think I would have gotten into the drug culture in San Francisco, but noooo, it took over twenty years later and a little thing called crack cocaine to make an addict out of me at the should of known better age of forty-five-- Bless Your Heart for thinking I would follow a logical path. I'm so right-brained that I can barely use an electric can opener. We right-brainers are the creative ones!!

I turned twenty one, right after I moved to San Francisco. The first legal drink I bought was a gin & tonic with two limes. My friend Sharon Lee Muscatel suggested that it was a good, basic drink for me and I could order it just about anywhere. I was glad for such uptown advice. I mean I was just a small town girl here in one of the most exciting cities in the world and I had just turned twenty-one. The fact that Sharon Lee had completely shaved her head the day before sort of had me wondering, but hey she convinced me with her heartfelt emotion. She said her aunt had cancer and Sharon Lee thought her aunt's head was beautiful and she knew that her own head was beautiful, so here she was with a shaved head that she intended to keep. Hey, it was 1981 in San Francisco and people were doing their own thing.

The next day at work at our ultra-conservative Law firm located in the pyramid building in the heart of the city, Sharon Lee arrived with her newly bald head. Our Human Resources administrator wasn't amused and she sent Sharon out to buy a wig. Today, that might be grounds for firing, but back then, we did what we were told.

Sharon invited me over to her apartment a couple of months later to meet her new husband!! I hadn't even known she was dating anyone. She wasn't really, she just explained that Ishman needed an American wife to stay in the country and she needed a little companionship. So, the little dinner party at Sharon's place was unique indeed. There were other wives there in flowing skirts and castanets, and Sharon had on a headpiece to cover her newly growing out hair. Sharon's fads seemed to come and go very quickly here. Hey Toto, we are definitely not in Kansas, anymore.

In Sharon's kitchen, I was propositioned by one of Isman's friends, Ackhmed. He pushed me up against the refrigerator and declared in <u>very</u>, <u>very</u> accented English,

"I like to make love with dogs."

Being the overly polite Grits (Girl Raised in the South) kind of girl I was, I thought he must have misspoken a preposition, and replied,

"Oh, you like to make love <u>like </u>a dog" I said pleasantly.

Sharon had just entered the kitchen and said,

" No, Meg they really do make love with dogs, you ought to see it!"
Sharon Lee Muscatel Mohammed exclaimed.

I said I'll pass and managed to leave somewhat gracefully exit from the kitchen.

Unknown to little ole naïve me from the South, these men were part of the Iranian controversy. It was 1981 and the Iran Contra hearings were going on—

SHRED, FAWN, SHRED, SAID OLIVER NORTH.

DOES ANYONE REMEMBER THIS T-SHIRT?

From that night on it was like a light went off around me announcing to all of the Iranian gentlemen in San Francisco, that yes, I was a born and breed true-blooded American Girl. I guess I do look quintessentially American-Blonde hair, green eyes. And because I have a friendly, easy-going smile, I was an easy target for these men who called themselves "Persians".

One particularly frightening incident happened as I crossed a street in San Francisco to the ACT (American Conservatory Theatre) to audition for a spot with their illustrious company. Two "Persian" men grabbed me as I walked across the crowded sidewalk and tried to drag me into a waiting car. I screamed and kicked and thankfully an American guy intervened and took me into a record store where he worked.

Breathless and on the edge of tears, I said,

"Thanks so much for helping me. What did they want?"

"To marry you and get their green card so they can stay in the United States", he answered. " They say they're Persians, yet they're really Iranians!"

"Yeah, I kind of thought Persia wasn't really a country anymore. How did they know I'm American? "

"Well, look at your blonde hair, green eyes. You're obviously American."

Darn it!! Yet another time when an ethnic look would have worked for me!!

Acupuncture in Chinatown

In order to cure my sinus problems, I went to see an acupuncturist in Chinatown. I loved Chinatown in San Francisco!! When I first moved to the Golden Gate city, I walked through Chinatown during the Christmas season and was surprised and delighted to hear "Santa Claus is coming to Town" with a Chinese accent playing in the stores.

I've always had a problem with my sinuses. It seems to me when I live where I'm surrounded by water, my sinus problems are even worse than usual. I constantly suffered with major sinus problems when I lived in San Francisco, California. A friend at work, Patty, suggested I visit a "Head Shop" to buy some nasal spray that was just salt and water. It was called "Nasal-ease". I didn't even know what a head shop was and she had to explain it to me. Only years later did I realize that the silver amulet that Patty wore around her neck had a silver spoon and white powder in it!! Ah, I miss the good ole naïve days!!

So I used my Nasal-ease and with my super fast way of talking and my constant sniffing with sinus problems didn't think a thing about it. In retrospect, I'm sure everyone in San Francisco thought I was a cocaine user. I didn't even understand it then. Unfortunately twenty some years later, I understood it all too well.

I really resent the loss of my "virginity" when it comes to drug knowledge. However, knowledge is power, and I do believe that I'm supposed to share with the world what I have learned from my introduction to drugs through my ex-husband. So, I'll get off my proverbial soap- box and hope my stories help. How very Zen!!!

In order to cure my sinus problems, Sharon Lee Muscatel Mohammed, of the "I like to Make Love with Dogs, husband fame", suggested that I get acupuncture. She gave me a card with an address on it in Chinatown and told me that Master Lee was a master at curing anything and everything.

And since Sharon had shaved her head bald and married a "Persian" to keep him in the country, I, of course followed her sage advice and ended up in Chinatown wandering the crooked streets trying to find the correct address of the wonderful Master Lee.

I entered the "Five Happy Family" Chinese restaurant and asked for Master Lee. I was asked if I had a card and I showed them the tattered business card from Sharon Lee Muscatel Mohammed.

The waiter said, "ah, Miss Sharon Lee—she is good customer."

Hmm, like I had any doubt! Sharon Lee always gave me good referrals, I thought smugly as I followed the waiter up some rickety back stairs. He led me to what appeared to be a doctor's waiting room, filled with Chinese ladies, Chinese children and a little old Chinese men with his pet bird in a small walking cage. There was an old apothecary medicine chest set-up behind the counter with many different herbs and an abacus right beside it. Wow, I was definitely in a different culture, for sure. This wasn't like the Piggly Wiggly's pharmacy back home.

I waited awhile in the middle of what looked like to me "The World of Suzie Wong" and then found myself behind a bamboo curtain rod on a table. Master Lee approached and spoke only Chinese, which of course I didn't understand. So I assumed he was asking me where it hurt. I pointed to my nose and forehead and did my best imitation of Felix Unger in "The Odd Couple" having a sinus attack. This impression seemed to translate from English to Chinese in a universal way and Master Lee began to put acupuncture needles in my nose.

Alrighty then, these needles weren't nearly as long as I had thought they would be. They were short like regular sewing needles. And to add to my delight---Master Lee put cork on the ends of the needles. He then lit a match to the cork and voila, I now had needles with a burning cork stuck into the sides of my nose.

As I lay there I noted a fascinating scientific fact—metal conducts heat!!! And as I was laying in a dark, back alley on a rickety bamboo bed in Chinatown in San Francisco, it occurred to me that maybe once again my friend, Sharon Lee Muscatel Mohammed, had perhaps led me down the wrong path. Hmm, you think?

Master Lee had also put needles with burning corks in my belly and I once again made the scientific connection—metal conducts heat!! I tried placing my hands between my skin and the needle and once again—metal conducted heat!! After five more long, long minutes of this Chinese healing torture, Master Lee removed the needles. I felt such relief from the burning that I let out a big sigh and also noticed that I could breathe much, much better. Hey, maybe there was something to this two thousand year old art. I breathed deeply again and felt great relief in my nose and my headaches seemed to have disappeared.

I was happy with this recent turn of events and returned to see Master Lee every couple of weeks for about a year and a half until I left San Francisco and moved to Atlanta.

CHAPTER SIX

ATLANTA

I left my heart in San Francisco and returned to the city of my birth, Atlanta. As you know,

I WAS BORN IN ATLANTA AND MY MOTHER'S NAME IS DIXIE.

I had a new job at a big law firm in downtown Atlanta. Newt Gingrich was one of the lawyers there. At that time he wasn't speaker of the house, just a sweet southern gentleman with a unique name. One of the firm's biggest clients was the WWWF (The World Wide Wrestling Federation) of Georgia. Now these guys were a fun group when they were in our conference room taking depositions with our Atlanta lawyers. These buffed-out guys who must have been on steroids, look almost like cartoon characters in their suits.

My receptionist desk was right outside the large conference room. This was 1981 so I had to place any long distance calls for the attorneys. I got to go in and out of the conference room frequently and delight in seeing the WWWF guys trying to look corporate. Close your eyes and imagine Rick Flair in a dark suit with a bright orange tie with palm trees on it. Are your eyes closed? Bless your heart, it was just like you would imagine!! It was a hoot! I was just a footstep away from show biz!

In my opinion, not all technology changes are for the good. At Kilpatrick & Cody law firm in Atlanta, Georgia there were no fax machines; so, cute, young guys and sometimes gals on bicycles delivered the myriad of paperwork necessary to keep a law firm running smoothly.

We had eight floors of law firm with a receptionist on each floor. My job was to be the relief receptionist; I gave the other receptionists their breaks and lunches. This sporadic schedule suited my ADHD personality—I got to see and be seen by all the attorneys and clients and I could quickly move on from one adventure to another.

A SORT OF METAPHOR FOR MY LIFE...

Claudette Butler was the head receptionist and she had been at Kilpatrick & Cody for over 15 years. That was a long, long time to a newly working twenty-three year old girl who was Dixie-Born (pun intended). Claudette always told me that she was true Atlanta royalty and that she was descended directly from Rhett Butler's people. I was young and gullible, so it only took me about six months to realize that Rhett Butler was a character from "Gone with the Wind" and the Butler name was fictitious, so Claudette couldn't really be kin to Rhett and Scarlett.

Hey, we southerners take our history very, very seriously, even if it is fiction. I mean Margaret Mitchell is an icon to the people of Atlanta!

My friend Claudette Butler would also attend a "Parents without Partners" meeting every Thursday night. She said they would have a meeting and then have refreshments and a dance. Claudette was always raving about what a wonderful time she had at these PWP meetings. Again, remember I was and still am somewhat gullible and naïve; therefore, I just assumed that since Claudette Butler had been married that she had children. Well bless her heart when I found out that Percy Butler was a six-year-old spoiled-rotten standard poodle.

CHAPTER SEVEN

MICHAEL JACKSON
AND THE BOY

I swear I am just one step away from stardom. You know that game "Six Degrees of Separation from Kevin Bacon"? Well, I am just one degree away from many different celebrities. I acted in a made for TV movie in Japan with Florence Griffith Joyner, I've appeared beside and sold books for Glenn Beck, Dave Barry, Ed Begley, Jr. and Winston Churchill, IV and many other New York Times best-selling authors.

I made a series of Japanese rock videos with Mikiko Noda, (the Carrie Underwood of Japan). I was directed in a play in Atlanta by Kenny Leon (Tony Award winner for "A Raisin in the Sun" on Broadway).We played at the Martin Luther King, Jr. Center for Non-Violent Social Change. Yolanda King and Freddy "Boom-Boom " Washington attended our opening and we partied with them afterwards. I performed as a Magician's Assistant and

Miami Dolphins, Bob Griese, and Frank Gifford, Kathie Lee's husband, wanted a photo taken with me.

So let's just say I've been One or Two Degrees away from stardom for a long time. I'm waiting for my big break; however, I'm happy with the way things are for me! Hey, Kathy Griffin, maybe I can be on the "D" list too!!

While I worked for the Muscular Dystrophy Association as a professional fundraiser and patient services coordinator, I lived a schizophrenic existence. One minute I would be on the phone with someone about sponsoring a golf tournament for "Jerry's Kids"—the next minute I would be consoling a patient who had just been diagnosed with terminal ALS, Lou Gehrig's disease.

I was privileged to work with about 300 patients who had been diagnosed with one of forty neuromuscular diseases. I coordinated the support groups and met many wonderful people—both adults and children, who sadly have left this world.

One young boy in particular captured my heart -- Bobby Harold, a twelve year old Navy Brat who had recently moved to Virginia Beach from California with his family. It was 1992 and Bobby and his mother, Stacy, delighted in telling me about when Bobby had appeared in the world famous music video, "We Are The World" in 1985 with Michael Jackson and so many famous people.

What a story they told about the making of that video. Michael Jackson, Stevie Wonder, Diana Ross, Cher, Quincy Jones and lots of Make A Wish kids. To be eligible to be a Make A Wish kid, you have to be considered terminally ill by your doctor. Many of our MDA kids received a Wish and Bobby Harold's had been to meet Michael Jackson.

Now, remember this was 1992 and the world knew nothing yet of Michael Jackson's reputation for being friends with young boys. That scandal would happen the next year, 1993.

Bobby and Stacy told me how Michael Jackson invited them to spend time at The Neverland Ranch. I heard all about the ferris wheel, Bubbles the chimp, the cotton candy and the sleepovers in Michael Jackson's room!! Bless your hearts, I am not kidding. I thought that the idea of young boys sleeping in Michaels Jackson's room was not a good idea and said so to Stacy, the Mom. She told me that she would drive Bobby to Neverland and leave him there alone for several days at a time.

Bobby Harold was twelve years old at the time. Once the scandal broke in 1993 I worried about Bobby and his friendship with Michael Jackson. I still wonder to this day what really happened and the story gets even more interesting.

The King of Pop married the King's Daughter. Yes, remember when Michael Jackson married Lisa Marie Presley? A match made in "Enquirer" heaven. And remember when Michael and Lisa Marie appeared on television in an interview with ABC's Diane Sawyer?

Like millions of Americans, Ned and I watched this interview with interest, delight and a lot of curiosity. Bobby Harold had told me that Michael Jackson wanted to publicly acknowledge him in this interview. I smiled and nodded and agreed with Bobby that would be fabulous!! Of course, I really didn't believe a word of it. This was just more of Bobby's daydreaming—or so I thought…

Well, you could have knocked me over with a feather! At the end of Michael Jackson and Lisa Marie Presley's interview with Diane Sawyer, Michael looked straight at the camera and said, "Hi, Bobby Harold"!!!!!

Ned and I gasped and said to each other,

"Oh my gosh, the kid has been telling the truth all along!
Not long after that Michael Jackson's album
<u>HIStory</u> came out and the song,
"Childhood" was dedicated to Bobby Harold.

I tell you, truth is stranger than fiction any day of the week. I swear, you just can't make this stuff up.

Bless Your Heart.

CHAPTER EIGHT

LOVE & MARRIAGE

Bless their hearts, small town America seems to have an overabundance of drug problems. The Meth Problem is especially prevalent in small towns. My theory is that hey, there's not much to do in a small town so drugs, sex and rock & roll are kind of like a trip to the mall for bigger city kids! Anyway, most of the kids that I grew up with in Martinsville, Virginia were into drugs in one form or another—drinking, smoking marijuana, snorting cocaine, and shooting up heroin.

One family friend in particular, Ned Waters, had a reputation for doing drugs and rumor had it that he even sold stuff right out of his parent's big, beautiful Tara-esque white house. I used to baby-sit for his younger brother and I did know that Ned had a drug problem.

In high school, I was so naïve at that time, that I really didn't even smoke cigarettes or smoke marijuana or even drink very much either. Hey remember I was "High on Life!!"

I used to think that I hadn't suffered enough in life to be a great actress—well, HELLO, REAL WORLD, I have suffered some now...and feel the need to tell my story to hopefully help someone else navigate the trials and tribulations of drug addiction.

Alrighty now, stay tuned and let's fast forward to my marriage to Ned Waters. That's right, the same Ned Waters who sold drugs out of his big, white house on the Lake where we both grew up. I had decided not to be a Southern Mafia Princess, so I chose someone to marry who was familiar to me. In fact, both of our cad Grandfathers cheated on our Southern Grandmothers and were drinking buddies together back in good ole' Martinsville-- so rumor had it.

In true Southern style, Ned and I were actually related—but hey just by marriage, so it really doesn't count, does it? We both had blonde hair and green eyes. You see-- my father's sister was married to his father's first cousin. We had double cousins! What a hoot! My first cousins were his second cousins. We used to kid that we were really from West Virginia and that's why we didn't have children. We didn't want to taint the gene pool, you know.

The truth is that Ned and I probably talked more about having children than most people do that actually have children. I had some fertility problems. It had taken my Mom five years to get pregnant and it took her sister eight years. I guess the women in my family weren't particularly fertile myrtles! Of course the mere fact that my husband was in the Navy and the fact that we had no sex life to speak of would have made getting pregnant difficult.

At one time we even looked into adopting an Asian infant. In Japan, unless the baby has both a Japanese mother and father, the baby is frowned upon and is usually put up for adoption. We both liked the idea of having an Asian little girl. Seeing a Japanese little girl in her school uniform with matching cap was an adorable sight.

True Confession time here—the real reason we didn't have children was that we rarely ever had relations. It has taken me over twenty years to figure this entire marriage out, and in retrospect I feel like a "dumb blonde". However, I truly believe that Ned was gay and in the military and he wanted to stay in and advance his career. So what was better to do than to marry an old family friend who was cute, funny and could be a beard for him?

I, on the other hand, was fresh from a relationship with someone's family who was Mafia; Doesn't this sort of stuff happen to you all the time? Well, bless your little pea-pickin hearts. It's always happening to me.

So good ole' Ned certainly seemed like a safe pick at the time. Hey I was 27 ½ and I didn't want to be an old maid! Plus—Join the Navy, See the World, I had always wanted to travel…

The true fact that Ned had a druggie background sort of entered my mind, but not really. I mean he had spent seven years in the Navy and had done very well. Unbeknownst to me he'd <u>had</u> to join the Navy to escape jail time for a drug conviction. Funny how the small details are the ones you should pay attention to—

Karma definitely was in the works on this one...

A Navy Chaplain from Missouri married us on February 20, 1988 in Virginia Beach, Virginia. The night before we got married, Ned got high with an old friend and stayed up all night partying with him. The next morning at our wedding breakfast his eyes were so red and bloodshot and I have lovely pictures to remember that by. And just before the wedding he took a fistful of Valium. And on our wedding night he didn't really want to make love; however, I insisted. This was indeed a bad way to start a marriage…hmm hindsight is definitely 20/20.

I should have wised up and realized that he was trying to escape from the marriage situation and his feelings. Isn't that why we all start to use or abuse something—to escape from our deepest feelings? I guess that's what addiction is all about--escaping and trying to cope by altering your mood.

HEY, THAT'S WHY THEY CALL THEM MOOD-ALTERING DRUGS, DON'T YOU THINK?

When I attended NA (Narcotics Anonymous) and AA(Alcholics Anonymous) meetings and heard the saying, "You're only as sick as your deepest secrets", I cried. I realized that by admitting the truth and speaking about what has happened to me too, I won't feel sick anymore…

<u>That</u> is why I am sharing my story, so <u>you</u> can realize that when you tell the truth, those deep, dark secrets <u>can't</u> hurt you anymore.

Of course, Ned also drank somewhat at the beginning of our marriage. Fast forward the years to a little later in the marriage and he would drink twelve to twenty beers a night, eat dinner, take a Jacuzzi, eat ice cream with Bert, our beloved, black Cocker Spaniel and then finally make it back to the bed.

> In retrospect, it is kind of ironic how many things
> he did to avoid being in bed with me!!

Of course, being a woman, I felt for years that I wasn't desirable enough. Hey I had never, ever had a problem with attracting guys. In fact, it was the exact opposite. Everyone I knew "came on" to me—Men, Women, Dogs –LOL! It took me years and years to realize that it was Ned's problem, not mine. He used to say these exact words "Meg, I can't help it if I'm not attracted to you." And finally after about ten years of marriage, I finally understood. He couldn't help it if he naturally didn't feel attracted to women or me. I mean I believe in the "nature versus nurture" theory. A person is born a certain way with certain sexual tastes and it stays the same throughout your lifetime.

When someone drinks on a daily basis, you definitely begin to notice his pattern. Ned's pattern was to drink about three beers within the first hour of coming home from work. He would usually be in a grouchy mood and then after three beers; he would be in a good mood. Imagine that!! Then the old Dr. Jekyll and Mr. Hyde character transformation would begin for the night. I would decide to skip this soap opera episode and retreat to the bedroom to escape his wraith. Looking back on things now, he could have been doing cocaine then also and I just didn't realize it. That might explain some of his very strange mood behaviors. Now, that I know more about which drug affects you in which way, I can't really say if Ned was using cocaine way back then or not.

I just know that it is very, very hard to live with someone who is addicted to drugs or alcohol.

I have a very easy-going, high-energy personality and I tend to cheerfully overlook things. For a long while I was definitely passive-aggressive in my relationship with Ned. I would smile and nod to him and then just do whatever I wanted to do. I see now that my behavior certainly contributed to our problems—Ned loved to debate an issue just for the fun of it-especially politics. Not wanting to make him angry, I would not take a strong stance on many things and it drove him crazy.

It was almost like living with Lucille Ball and Archie Bunker. We weren't on the same time frame, heck we weren't even in the same decade!! One time I caught our microwave on fire. Hey, who knew that Arby's wraps their sandwiches in metal paper??? Well, I sure didn't!! At home for a quick lunch before I had to go back to work, I popped the whole Arby's bag in the Microwave to warm up.

Well, I noticed a little spark and unwittingly added oxygen to the fire by jerking open the door. Flames burst out and I slammed the microwave door. Flames were still igniting and luckily I remembered we had a fire extinguisher, which I pointed at the microwave like a gun, all the time trying to pull the trigger. Hey, as I found out later, you're supposed to pull the black thing out. Who knew?? Finally the fire went out and the expensive microwave over the stove was ruined and the heating element inside was melted like the wicked witch in the Wizard of Oz when she has water thrown on her.

I called Ned at work to warn him and told him that I'd had a little accident with the microwave, but it was nothing serious! For years, Ned would tell a great story while we both acted out our parts in pantomime. Picture me trying to put out the fire using the extinguisher as a gun in a business suit and high heels.

What a hoot! Ned would say, "Thank God she didn't know how a fire extinguisher works or I'd have to clean up that mess too! And Ned's funniest line was "and she even left the damn ketchup packets in the bag!!!

In many ways, Ned and I understood each other! I was the positive energy and he knew how to focus my energy. I loved nothing better than hearing him tell that story-over and over! I was the yin to his yang. So in many ways our marriage worked for us.

I was truly marrying the boy next door. Well, to be technical, the boy across the lake. A big, beautiful man-made lake was in the middle of our neighborhoods and Ned's big, white house was right on the water. I was one block off the Lake on the other side, however when I crossed the street to get our mail I always looked across the lake to their beautiful family home.

I used to baby sit Ned's little brother and even went on family vacations with his Mom, sister and younger brother and my Mom and younger brother. Naturally being a cool teenager at the time, Ned didn't go on these trips.

Ned's Mom really liked me, and years later when I became her daughter-in-law, we got along wonderfully. Ned's father was a best friend to my father and unfortunately, his father died when Ned was only seventeen. I do believe that his father's death hastened Ned's trip down Strawberry Lane. Losing a parent is difficult at any age; however this age is especially tough and Ned was looking to escape. And Ned's escape was drugs and alcohol, just like it was for so many other baby-boomers.

CHAPTER NINE

JAPAN

When I married Ned I was so excited about the whole "Join the Navy, See the World" concept. We had only been married less than a year when he had orders coming up for a change of station. Ned knew of my wanderlust and he too liked to travel the world. Ned told me that we could go up to the Pentagon and see his recruiter in person and I could charm the guy into sending us wherever I wanted to go. So, naturally I put on a short skirt and a tight t-shirt and off we went to the Pentagon to convince Ned's detailer to send us overseas.

We had wanted to go to Italy; however, the detailer (Navy guy who gives you job assignments) seemed to think Yokosuka, Japan would be a very exciting place for us to live. Quicker than Ned or I could blink an eye, I rattled off his social security number to the guy at the Pentagon with his fingers poised over the keyboard.

I paused a split second as I looked at Ned and said,
"Well how about Japan, that sounds like fun!!"
And Ned nodded yes.

We didn't know that to be stationed in Yokosuka, Japan meant that you were "forward deployed". This meant that Ned and all the other sailors would be gone about six months to sea and back home on shore only for approximately six weeks, then they would deploy again for another six months. If they were lucky, they could remain on land for six weeks, the sea life would be call them again and on and on. It was a really tough way for both the sailors and their "dependents", as the Navy calls women and children, to live.

The first Iraq war began at this time and Ned was on the USS Fife and located just miles off the Saudi Arabian coast. He told me that his ship shot more tomahawk missiles than any other ship in the war. Ned was the weapons control officer so I can only imagine what stress that was for him.

He also told me that he could see Saddham Hussein's oil fields being burned just by looking at them with the naked eye. They were only about a mile away. The USS Fife was hovering over some mines or bombs in the sea for about three days. Ned was the Operations Specialist in charge of navigating the ship very stealthily at this time. He said it was so very different from what you would expect <u>WAR</u> to be. It was silent and his palms sweat and everyone in the Combat Information Center was deadly quiet. Wow, how frightening!

One time during Operation Desert Storm, the USS Fife was due back in port for their six weeks shore stay and the wives and children and Bert, our black cocker spaniel, were waiting on the pier in Yokosuka, Japan for the ship to dock. The ship never did dock and it turned around in the water and headed back to defend America's freedom. It was a very sad sight for the dependents. We didn't see our loved ones again for another four months.

They do say, "Being a Navy Wife is the toughest job in the world" and on that day I would have to agree.

I actually loved being a Navy Wife. Ned used to say that I should do public relations for the Navy. Ironically, I now do public relations for a living. I can sell ice to Eskimos, especially if I believe in the cause.

I loved the way the Navy was there for you to have in the background if something happened overseas that you couldn't quite handle, like forgetting your passport when you are trying to fly back home on Christmas Eve when your husband is at war...yet, another crazy story to be confessed later...

CHAPTER TEN

BACK HOME TO MARTINSVILLE TO DIXIE & BAILEY

It was 1985 and I had left Atlanta to move back home to take care of my mother, Dixie, who had breast cancer and had a mastectomy. My mom was definitely a trooper during this entire nightmare of chemotherapy, hair loss and constantly feeling sick. I had left Atlanta and the Mafia behind me (I thought) to come home and take care of my fabulous Mom.

They definitely broke the mold when my Mom, Dixie, was created. My Mom has a fabulous never met a stranger personality that I have inherited. She has a strong spirit with a love of life that is a joy to experience. Her self-confidence and energy level have given me quite an example to live up to.

Needless to say, when this vibrant and high-energy redhead became sick and wheelchair bound, it broke my heart.

One of my favorite memories of my Mom is when I was in college and about to go home for my first visit since being away. She called me excitedly and told me,

"Wait until you see the entrance foyer!!
I've re-wallpapered the hall in
Lesbian nudes and peacocks!!"

That's my Mom!!!

So, when Mom was diagnosed with breast cancer, I left my job at the law firm, left the Academy Theatre and left Alberto Romano to go home and look after Dixie.

So, in 1986 I moved back home to take care of my Mom who was recovering from breast cancer surgery. Dixie is a survivor in the best sense of the word. She is a spunky, high energy red-head who approaches life with a zest that I truly envy. I like to think I have inherited this spunky, 'Life is too short to drink cheap wine' attitude.

So when Mom was diagnosed with breast cancer, I left my job at the law firm, left the Academy Theatre and Alberto Romano to go home and look after Dixie.

My Dad's name is Bailey and he is the quintessential southern gentleman. Think of Dick Van Dyke and you'll get a wonderful picture of Bailey Henderson. Silver hair with blue eyes and tall and thin, my father is quite a looker. Add his charming personality and wry sense of humor and he is a delight to behold.

My Dad is a frustrated entertainer and loves to sing. For a man who is eighty, Bailey Henderson is very computer literate. Bailey constantly downloads music from all eras onto his computer.

From Hoagie Carmichael's "Stardust" to
David Bowie's "Fame" to Diana Krall's Jazz,
my Dad knows all the tunes!

Bailey Henderson is such a warm, easy-going soul and I like to think I have definitely inherited his kind nature and deep-down goodness.

BACK HOME TO MARTINSVILLE, VIRGINIA

SO IN 1986 I MOVED BACK HOME TO TAKE CARE OF MY MOM. AS THOMAS WOLFE SAYS, "YOU CAN'T GO HOME AGAIN"

And alas, it is <u>so</u> true. Once you have ventured from home and out of your comfort zone for the first time, your eyes on the world are forever changed.

When I first moved to San Francisco from Martinsville, Virginia and Boone, North Carolina, I was so self-conscious about my southern accent.

My older brother, Jim, lived in San Francisco and when I met his friends, they all told him,

"I can't understand a word she is saying!
All I hear is yada, yada, yada, y'all".

When I heard this I was determined to try and hide my small town southernisms. I had turned twenty-one when I moved to San Francisco and was desperately trying to be more cosmopolitan. Looking back on this, I see that one of life's

Best pieces of advice comes from
Mr. William Shakespeare.

"To thine own self be true."

It took me many years to realize this and now at forty-nine, I am so much more comfortable in my own skin. Thanks Mr. Shakespeare.

> "Wow, as <u>they</u> say—
> Youth really is wasted on the young."

And who is <u>THEY</u> anyway? There must be an ancient philosopher named <u>THEY</u> who said many, many deep philosophical things and he continues to be quoted today. So next time you hear someone quote, <u>THEY</u> say---just smile knowingly to yourself and know that you are in on a very, very old secret.

BACK HOME TO DIXIE & BAILEY

So I had left Atlanta and moved back home to take care of my mother who had breast cancer. It was a difficult time for my family. My Mom was being given chemotherapy drugs and if the cancer didn't kill her, we thought the chemo treatments just might.

Dixie had many strange reactions to the chemotherapy. It kills the bad cells and unfortunately some of the good cells too. Mom had drug- induced Parkinson symptoms. Her legs would involuntarily tap on the foot pedals of her wheelchair.

> "Hey, I'm the tap dancer in the family,"
> I'd say and we would both laugh.
> That is one of the best lessons I
> Ever learned from both
> My parents.
> Laughter is the Best Medicine.

Her fingertips were numbed by one of the drugs and she would fall asleep in the middle of a conversation. There were also other puzzling side effects. Chemotherapy is such a dicey move. You roll the dice and hope that the outcome is for the best.

I would wheel her around the house while we cleaned things up and purged my younger brother, Christopher's, room of magazines and other assorted stuff. Mom would tap dance a little with her feet and I would make a comment and then she would immediately fall asleep. It was very sad for me, yet my Mom was still alive and I felt very happy about that.

It was 1986 and for some crazy reason---
Coca-Cola decided to change their formula
And call it 'New Coke'.

October 21, 1986

Dear Coca Cola Marketing Dept 101,

I know hindsight is 20/20 and I know America hadn't experienced the equally bad public relations fiasco of Monica Lewinsky as the spokeswoman for Jenny Craig, but hey you know what

THEY say…

"Is nothing sacred anymore?
Change the original formula
Of Coca-Cola?"

Sincerely,

A Former Customer

I can see some marketing guy coming up with an idea to impress his boss; however, did the Coca-Cola marketing team realize that…

IF IT AIN'T BROKE, DON'T FIX IT!!!

My mom and I began to hoard Coca-Cola in our basement. We ordered the fabulously wonderful eight ounce cokes from our local Coca-Cola distributor and kept them cool in the basement. We would only drink them sparingly because we knew the end was coming soon---no more Coca-Cola as we knew it. Remember I was born in Atlanta, so Coca-Cola had been served in my baby bottles. Dixie and I were very frugal with our beloved coca-colas.

CHAPTER ELEVEN

LIFE ISN'T ALL IT'S CRACKED UP TO BE

I had been married to Ned Waters for seventeen years and should have left him after ten years of marriage. Of course hindsight is 20/20. You know what <u>THEY</u> say…

In October of 2005, my life was about to take
a huge turn for the worse and I didn't even know it.

Gee, there should have been some sort of a sign.
You know, stop-yield-caution…

Or like in the Wizard of Oz,
"I'd turn back if I were you."

Ah, but life doesn't spell itself out when we are in the middle of it. It flows along like a winding road and we don't see the twists and turns that we should obviously take. We just keep flowing along and destiny takes over and the route is set in stone whether we know it or not and we are propelled forward down the wrong road.

I don't believe in coincidences, I believe in 'God Winks' and that things are meant to happen and if we pay attention to them, we will be on the right path. However, if we act on automatic pilot and ignore our internal compass, we will always, always end up heading in the wrong direction.

All my life I had followed my own inner compass and marched to the beat of my own drummer and somehow managed to always follow <u>MY</u> right path,

HOWEVER,
IN OCTOBER OF 2005, I IGNORED MY
INNER COMPASS AND TRIED TO
MAKE MY MARRIAGE WORK.

WOW, WHAT A LIFE-CHANGING MISTAKE I MADE
AS I HEADED BLINDLY DOWN THE ROAD
WITH MY USUAL,
'READY, FIRE, AIM' PERSONALITY.
JUMPING INTO SOMETHING
WITHOUT THINKING...

Ned had done drugs when he was a teen-ager. He had used and sold drugs and he had even needed to join the Navy to avoid jail time. Now I knew this and in retrospect (darn, that 20/20 vision), I should have been more alert to the possibility that he might have a midlife crisis and go to doing what made him happy when he was seventeen---drugs...

He had already bought a snappy, silver BMW Z3 convertible and that seemed to make him a little happier. Ned's midlife crisis was about to spiral out of

Control

And

Take

Me

Down

With

It.

It was right before Halloween of 2005 and Ned and I were finally honest with each other about how unhappy we had been. We talked about splitting up and he was ready to leave the house and leave everything to me—or so he said...

What I didn't know at the time was that Ned had been doing crack cocaine for about a year before I ever realized it. In fact, I wouldn't have ever known if he hadn't offered me some. He didn't tell me what it was, he just said here, smoke this, I think you'll like this.

Now, remember I was a get high on life kind of gal so my experience with drugs had been limited to smoking marijuana in college. I hadn't liked it then because it made me paranoid. Since I don't smoke cigarettes, marijuana made me cough terribly. I had snorted cocaine in the 1980's once and thought it was kind of fun, yet the teeth grinding tension was not fun for me. That was it for me and recreational drugs.

Ned and I had been chatting about lots of things openly for the first time in a very long time. He said hey, I've got something I think you might like. He handed me a silver pipe and I naively, stupidly smoked it.

The feeling was fast and fabulous! I had an instant orgasm! Now this was a feeling I could get used to. It made me feel like myself, yet better—it felt like me—happy & hyper. It was a good feeling…

The stop sign should have appeared and the
Green Police Nazi sirens should have sounded.

I wish the flying monkeys from the Wizard of Oz
Had come to fly me back home.

I KNEW I MADE A MUCH BETTER DOROTHY
THAN A WICKED WITCH,
I KNEW THERE WAS
"NO PLACE LIKE HOME"

I knew who I was and didn't need to get high and <u>YET I DID</u>. If there is one single, solitary, soulful lesson to be learned from my mistake, let it be-

**AS DYLAN THOMAS SAID,
"DO NOT GO GENTLE INTO
THAT GOOD NIGHT—
RAGE, RAGE AGAINST THE DYING
OF THE LIGHT."**

I should have paid attention to my inner voice, I knew it was such a stupid thing, yet I was trying to do something to bond with Ned and drugs were what brought us together and tore us apart and eventually ended Ned's life.

AH, ONCE AGAIN BEHOLD THE POWER OF HINDSIGHT...

CHAPTER TWELVE

MY LESSONS LEARNED

I have always learned life's toughest lessons the hard way. I have always learned from great literature by reading about others' feelings and it helps me to put my own feelings in perspective. So maybe talking about Dylan Thomas and "rage, rage against the dying of the light" is a little dramatic. Have you been reading my story? I mean the phrase DRAMA QUEEN has certainly been thrown in my direction once or twice!!

Don't rain on my parade, don't let the turkeys get you down, don't smoke crack cocaine!!! You would think these things would have been glaring obvious to **MOI.**

I definitely take responsibility for my own actions. I should not have naively, stupidly smoked whatever Ned gave me. I should have been true to myself. I should have just screamed,

JUST SAY NO...

It sounds trite and simple, yet I believe that this phrase means so much more and it has become my mantra. I am on a crusade to educate the public about the dangers of crack cocaine and how easily, needlessly, it can destroy your life. Hey, if it can happen to me, it can happen to anybody.

<u>I guess the world needs to be able to put a realistic face on addiction. So, I will be the new face of crack cocaine addiction. If it can happen to someone like me, it can happen to anyone.</u>

I smoked it once and was instantly addicted. And, if by being open and honest, I can make someone think twice and "Just Say No", then it's an important thing for me to do.

I was naïve about drugs and of all the experiences I'd had in the past, none of them had ever caused me to become addicted. I could drink two drinks and then switch to Diet Dr Pepper with no problem. I had smoked Mary Jane and never even liked it. I had snorted cocaine in the 1980's and it never became a habit. So when Ned offered me something to smoke, I did it, just because it seemed like fun. I guess that is the lesson to be learned from my mistake,

THINK
BEFORE YOU
DO
DRUGS, SEX AND ROCK & ROLL

So, for about nine months I was totally addicted to crack cocaine. I just reread that sentence and it does seem like I'm talking about someone else, not me. Yet, I must accept that I was addicted and I must be very careful not to fall down that rabbit hole again. Like Alice in Wonderland, I have a very inquisitive spirit and I will follow my curiosity, just like Alice followed the White Rabbit…

> Oh wow, didn't Lewis Carroll write
> Alice in Wonderland while
> Under the influence
> Of drugs?

> Hmm, interesting…
> That I chose this analogy,
> Or did it choose me?

At first doing the cocaine was so much fun!! I guess that's how it reels you in like a trout to a juicy worm. You have fun and don't even think about the consequences. At least I didn't. I was me—happy, hot and hyper, yet even more amplified. I talk very fast for a typical Southerner. When I was on "sparkle" as I chose to nickname it…I talked even faster—like the guy in the Federal Express commercials. After a few months of this, Ned and our friends who we partied with told me I should do downers to calm down. I guess I was even too hyper for other crack cocaine users.

CHAPTER THIRTEEN

SAVING PRIVATE MEG RYAN

I ran home to my parents, Dixie and Bailey. Boy, I've had lousy marriages; however, I have been blessed with great parents. When I left Ned, I didn't really realize that I would be leaving for good. I had a very bad mosquito bite on my eye after I woke up from a nap and my right eye was swollen badly. I showed Ned and in his typical Dr. Jekyll/Mr. Hyde personality, he told me I was fine and consoled me and then about fifteen minutes later he told me how stupid I was and how I was over reacting. He told me to leave and not to come back. After I arrived at my parents' house, Mom called Ned and told him I would be spending the night at their house and they would take me to Dr. LeHew's the next day for my eye.

Dixie, said, "Ned, it looks like a bad bug bite."

Ned replied, "Well, Dixie, if you think that, then
You can just f***ing keep her.

And Dixie said, "Well, now, I'm going
To do just that."

I was so glad to feel safe and away from the house that had become such a scary place for me to be. Hurricane Isabelle had flooded our house and our neighborhood had FEMA trailers all over it because our community had been more destroyed by the hurricane than any other neighborhood in Virginia Beach, Virginia.

I had been having terrible skin trouble and was itching terribly. Now, I am a very fair blonde with green eyes and my mother is a redhead, so it wasn't unusual for me to have skin problems; however something was really, really wrong. I didn't know it at the time; yet, I found out years later that the FEMA trailers were contaminated with formaldehyde! So, of course, I was having a reaction to these horrible chemicals.

At the time, as I told Ned and our friends how strange and weird I was feeling, none of them believed me and they tried to make me think I was going crazy. I was begging for help and said to them,

"Please , just take me to a hospital and drop me off. You
don't have to stay, I understand that you don't want to
stop doing crack cocaine, but I do and I need help."

I said to them,
"What are you trying to do to me? Gaslight me?"

I was referring to the Angela Lansbury movie, "Gaslight" where a woman is made to believe she is crazy by seeing gaslights dim and no one else will admit to seeing them.

It is a classic movie buff's line…"What are you trying to do?
Gaslight me?

They knew what I meant and just like in the movie,
they all made me believe I was crazy.

Sadly, it was two to three years later before I found out about the FEMA formaldehyde trailers contaminating my house. I felt a little vindicated; however, I just felt really sad that my friends wouldn't believe me and what a pitiful mess that my life had become from crack cocaine.

It has been three years now and I am only now—able to feel like I have gotten <u>me </u>back. Saving Private Meg Ryan has been a big job for me and I am so happy and thankful to have the Old Meg back.

Addiction makes you become someone you don't even recognize and definitely wouldn't want to be friends with.

After seeing Dr. Karen LeHew, I confessed to her that I felt that I was going to die. I told her about my crack cocaine use and said I needed help. She is also my Mom's family doctor and she trained at Eastern Virginia Medical School where my best friend and roommate, Jennie Jonnet, worked.

Susie Cummings, Dr. LeHew's nurse was also very kind and loving in my reaching out for help with my addiction.

Dr. LeHew Called Maryview Hospital in Portsmouth, Virginia and my Mom and Dad took me there. It was very, very hard for me to tell my Mom & Dad that I had been using cocaine. I realize now that it wasn't a big secret. There was a gigantic pink elephant in the room and I just wanted to let her out in the open and acknowledge that she was real!

Remember I had gone from a Marilyn Monroe figure to looking like Nicole Richey at her thinnest, in her over-sized sunglasses. It was quite evident that something was wrong with me…

We all thought I would be admitted to Maryview Hospital and have to stay for a couple of days or maybe a month. I was prepared and as I was questioned by a nurse about my problems, I asked,

"Is this where all the white, Upper middle class Crack whores go?"

I actually thought that there was such a place that women like me could go and get help. I was surprised and very disappointed to find out that no such place exists.

As the nurse laughed at my naïve question, she said,
"Honey, all we've got here are court ordered
People. They come here instead of jail."

And I replied,
"Where do women like me go for help?"

She shrugged and said, "Well, according to
Medical insurance, crack cocaine isn't addictive!"

I couldn't believe it...I had been honest and cried out for help and there really was no help for me. I knew I was addicted...yet...thank God, and I so very desperately needed help.

This is why I am here, telling you my story. I know that I wasn't the only upper middle class woman to have this problem. I see women everyday and I know they are using cocaine. I can tell by their eyes darting around frantically and praying no one notices that they aren't making direct eye contact and that they are paranoid.

I can tell

by the unhappiness

In

Their

Souls…

CHAPTER FOURTEEN

MY LIFE AS AN ADDICT

I was that skinny, bug-eyed paranoid middle class
woman who was afraid that the 'real world'
would find out my deep and darkest secret:

I WAS A CRACK COCAINE ADDICT.

Wow, what a long, long road it's been, Jerry Garcia. Oh by the way, I do love, love, love Ben & Jerry's new flavor of ice cream, "Cherry Garcia". Sorry, my ADD sometimes gets in the way of serious talk...

You could have knocked me over with a feather both literally and figuratively. I love to take a nightly bath to relax and have been doing so all my life. My life was so very different now—there was very little routine left. Yet, I still liked my nightly bath ritual and found comfort in it.

I have always had a voluptuous figure. I mean comparisons to Marilyn Monroe have been made about me. "Baby's got back" has also been said of my figure. So to find myself so very pathetically thin with no body fat whatsoever was a shock. I had to put towels in the bottom of the bathtub so I could take a bath without hurting my bony butt. That is when I realized how much I had changed and it was definitely not a change for the better.

I became paranoid about so many things—especially bugs and worms. I had developed such a fear of bugs, worms and things. I was definitely verging on paranoia. Yet when you are having these delusions, they are so very, very real. I truly believed that there were bugs on the pizza I had cooked and that my toothpaste was contaminated with parasites.

I read on the internet about a disease called "Morgellons" and there was definitely some similarities with my situation and other people who suffer from this disease. Many people who have been diagnosed with Morgellons had been living in places that had flooded such as Florida, New Orleans and Texas. Just like Hurricane Isabelle had ruined parts of my neighborhood in Chesapeake, Virginia right on the Intra Coastal Canal.

Yet, Morgellons has a definite stigma attached to it and many people suffering from it are considered delusional. The Center for Disease Controls in Atlanta says Morgellons disease still remains a medical mystery. So, of course, the drama queen inside of my cocaine-fueled brain totally believed that I had Morgellons and there were bugs inside my body trying to get out.

It is a known fact that cocaine users have bug paranoia. So my insistence that I saw bugs everywhere was definitely getting on Ned's nerves!!! Yet to Ned's credit, he was concerned that I wasn't eating at all now. I couldn't even swallow the rice in Campbell's Chicken with Rice soup. Between the constant crack cocaine cuisine and Morgellons mania, I was afraid to eat anything at all. I was down to eighty-eight pounds and giving Nicole Richey a run for her money.

Ned called Dixie and asked her if I could eat dinner with them. He told her I wasn't eating because I was convinced that there were bugs, parasites and worms in our house because of the floods from Hurricanes Floyd and Isabelle. So my Mom and Dad dutifully cooked dinner for me and watched as I ate tiny amounts of food and tried to make small talk with them.

A typical night for me and Ned would begin when he came home from work and I would finally fall into the bed to sleep maybe a few hours. On weekends, we hardly ever slept at all.

So when I would go to my parents for dinner, I had been awake doing crack cocaine for days. My mom's a great cook; however, I didn't have much of an appetite due to my current unhealthy lifestyle. So when my agitated body finally got some food and nutrition, I would fall asleep shortly after I ate. Luckily I lived five minutes away from them.

CHAPTER FIFTEEN

MY MID-LIFE CRISIS

THEY (REMEMBER HIM?) SAY THAT MOST OF AMERICANS MID-LIFE CRISIS, TAKE US BACK TO A TIME,

"WHEN WE WERE JUST SEVENTEEN AND YOU KNOW WHAT I MEAN."

ODE TO THE BEATLES...

We tend to long for a time when our lives were more carefree and simple and we had our whole lives in front of us. We baby boomers all have our mid-life in one form or another. My reaction to my own mid-life crisis was that I needed to know that I was still attractive to the opposite sex, since my husband never seemed to desire me. It took me over ten years and a very good psychiatrist—Thanks Dr. Sarah Moore—to realize that it wasn't really sex that I craved—it was to be desired, wanted and lusted after. That's what was missing in my life.

I had never had a problem attracting the opposite sex. But, news flash, after years of therapy with Dr. Sarah Moore, I finally understood the whole sad truth. Ned wasn't attracted to me because he wasn't attracted to anyone of the opposite sex. He was attracted to someone of the same sex.

Eureka, what a psychological break through!

I finally understood that my husband didn't desire any women, not just me. So I felt somewhat better, yet I was still feeling undesired and depressed.

Ned's mid-life crisis took a very different turn from mine. When he was "just seventeen", he was doing drugs and driving a sports car. And wow, big surprise, at the age of fifty, Ned went back to doing drugs and driving a BMW Z3 sports car.

I found out all about his drug use about four years after he had started using again. We both worked fulltime. Ned worked as a GS-12 in charge of top secret ships and traveled extensively around the world. Of course, he took these trips on his own and I never asked any questions. You know the Navy's policy, "don't ask, don't tell"? Well, I didn't ask questions about his travels because as you know, "loose lips, sink ships". Gee, I'm just full of Navy sayings, aren't I?

Anyway, years later Ned told me that he had taken a rock of crack cocaine with him to Singapore right in his pocket on a plane. He was scared he might be caught and exhilarated when he wasn't caught. This happened about a year and a half before I knew he was doing drugs again. I say again because when Ned was

JUST SEVENTEEN AND YOU KNOW WHAT I MEAN...

He had been very actively using drugs like marijuana, cocaine and heroin. This was the 1970's back in our boring little hometown of Martinsville, Virginia. And I do have a theory that drugs are more prevalent in small towns because there isn't much else to do. Ned was the perfect candidate to have a mid-life crisis.

He had just retired from twenty one years in the Navy and for the first time in a long time he would not be subjected to a drug test. He was bored with his life, and wondered like that old Peggy Lee song—'Is that all there is?' He was way over due for a mid-life crisis. He bought a beautiful silver BMW Z3 convertible and he seemed to get a kick out of driving it. That and his twenty-six foot Mariah speed boat docked in the backyard should have been enough.

Yet, we Americans never seem to have enough, do we?

TO QUOTE CARRIE FISHER, "INSTANT GRATIFICATION TAKES TOO LONG!!"

So, like so many of us baby boomers, Ned Waters needed to feel alive, like he was a vital part of the universe. So he turned back to what he had done

WHEN HE WAS JUST SEVENTEEN.

He went back to drugs. He told me that he had gone down to the Ocean View section of Norfolk, Virginia—a known drug hang out. He was driving along in his silver BMW Z3 and stopped a girl along the sidewalk and asked her where he could get something to smoke and,

Ned said, "Where can I get something to smoke?"

And she said, "White or green?"

And he said, "What do you mean smoking white?"

And she replied, "Come with me and I'll show you."

And the rest is history. I'm not really sure when this incident happened,
But, I believe it was in the spring of 2004.

By the fall of 2005, Ned had introduced me to crack cocaine, by handing
me a pipe and saying, "Here, smoke this. I think you'll like it."

Like a fool, I naively took the pipe and smoked it.
There should have been a sign to stop me from
Such stupidity!! I know to

"JUST SAY NO"

I should have paid attention to my inner compass.
Yet I was following Ned's lead and it
Definitely lead me in
The wrong direction.

CHAPTER FIFTEEN

THE TRUTH, THE WHOLE TRUTH & NOTHING BUT THE TRUTH

This chapter in particular has been very difficult for me to even begin to write. There is so much that I have told about the nine months of my life as a crack cocaine addict. And being a normal human being with morals and a conscious, I feel ashamed that all of this crazy stuff happened to me.

However, as THEY (remember him?) say in Narcotics Anonymous,

""YOU'RE ONLY AS SICK AS YOUR SECRETS."

The party had begun and I was up and running. It was definitely a party and lots of fun at first. I guess that's why people do drugs—it's fun, it's a release and it's recreational.

For the first time ever in our marriage, Ned and I related on a sexual level. Crack cocaine is a very powerful drug and makes you feel very turned on. We rented porno movies and I became introduced to a whole new world. With my own theatrical background, I was fascinated by the actors and actresses. I would google Jenna Jamison, Evan Hunter and other favorites of mine and learn all about their backgrounds. I had a new hobby! Ned and I became quite the movie buffs and we spent a lot of time watching these flicks.

I was losing a lot of weight and that is a definite side effect of crack cocaine use. In a matter of months I went from a Jennifer Lopez—Jenny from the block booty to a too thin Kelly Ripa wanna-be without the muscle tone. It was fun going back to my old sizes, the size six, the size four, the size two.

However, when I started to have to shop in the little girl's department and my voluptuous figure transformed into a skinny parody of its former self, I became concerned.

The crack cocaine made me so dry mouthed that I couldn't eat or swallow anything. It got to the point where I could only eat chicken with rice soup. But then, it became impossible for me to even swallow the rice!!

I couldn't eat, I wouldn't eat and I didn't eat. What with staying awake for days at a time and not eating, I became a member of a club that I never wanted to belong to. I yearned to live in the past where I could eat with abandon and actually enjoy my food. I had always had a voracious appetite and this was definitely,

A HORSE OF A DIFFERENT COLOR.

AND TO QUOTE MY FAVORITE SONG FROM "THE WIZARD OF OZ"

WE GET UP AT TWELVE AND START TO WORK AT ONE, TAKE AN HOUR FOR LUNCH AND THEN AT TWO, WE'RE DONE. JOLLY, GOOD FUN!!

Well welcome to yet another charming side effect of my personality, drifting off into other worlds seems infinitely more interesting or maybe it is my own ADD personality. Whatever it is, I do like to break into song and dance at the craziest moments. I've been told that I can be "utterly endearing" and "incredibly annoying" all at the same time.

So picture someone with a super high-energy personality and a Broadway show background being high on crack cocaine for nine months. It was enough to drive anyone crazy. Our friends and Ned all told me that I needed to do barbiturates or downers to calm down.

I said, 'Who wants to calm down?"

And they all said in unison, "We want you to.."

Well, it was time for me to make a drastic change and
Save my own life. As I found my truth, I found
Myself once again.

So that's my story and I'm sticking to it. I am going "Out on a Limb" like Shirley Maclaine and confessing my tales of crack cocaine addiction in order to motivate other addicts who need help. And also to educate people that it can happen to any one of us.

TREASURE YOUR LIFE,
LIVE YOUR DREAMS,
JUST SAY NO.
SLOGANS TO LIVE BY AND
TO MOTIVATE YOU.

Invite me to come speak at your school,
Your church, your NA & AA Meetings
And I will
Be sure to
Make you laugh,
Make you cry
As I tell you my—

CONFESSIONS
OF A SOUTHERN
BABY BOOMER.

www.ingramcontent.com/pod-product-compliance
Lightning Source LLC
Chambersburg PA
CBHW020350290526
45785CB00005B/2221